How can you sway the reader to feel like you desire them to feel?

Write a one page summary of your book.

"From Ordinary to ExtraOrdinary Author!"

Introduction

Today is the first day of the rest of your life. It is this day that you have decided to change your life forever. By purchasing this book, you have placed yourself on a course to completing your dream. RATHSI Publishing has created a seamless system that will focus your writing skills and enhance your book concept.

RATHSI Publishing was born from a frustrated author who had become feed up with the publishing industry. This industry has become so corporate and heartless that the true existence of publishing has taken a back seat.

RATHSI Publishing has created a systematic approach to the publishing process that releases the book we all have inside of us. By following these simple steps, you can develop a perfected manuscript and release that author in you.

It's up to you now to complete the following pages and begin fulfilling your dreams of being a published author.

Sincerely,

Patrick S. Muhammad, President of RATHSI Publishing

RATHSI

Describe the thoughts of the readers after they

complete your book.

Write a 5 sentence radio commercial for your book.

Describe your purpose for writing this book.

Sketch the cover of the book.

Write the chapter titles of your book.

Name the book.

Explain the name of the book.

Describe how the title relates to the summary, radio commercial, chapters, and you.

Rewrite the title of the book.

Describe your target audience of the book.

Interview yourself as if you are a member of that target audience. Create 1 question per chapter title explaining the chapter.

Rewrite the title of the book.

Re-sketch the cover of the book.

Rewrite the summary of the book.

Compile the cover and title.

"From Ordinary to ExtraOrdinary Author!"

Notes

It's now time to call RATHSI Publishing. You have completed this booklet because of your urgent desire to complete the book in you. Please fill out the form below or register online and claim your free copyright.

Free Copyright Once you join the RATHSI Publishing family.

Please forward all your contact information to: info@rathsipublishing.com

Name:

_____

Company:

_____

Address:

_____

Email: _____

City, State, Zip Code:

_____

Phone:

_____

"From Ordinary to ExtraOrdinary Author!"

RATHSI Publishing, LLC

2440 Fairburn Rd., Suite 101

Atlanta, GA 30331

www.rathsipublishing.com

info@rathsipublishing.com

(404) 207-0544

www.ingramcontent.com/pod-product-compliance
Lightning Source LLC
Chambersburg PA
CBHW070756050426
42449CB00010B/2500